Poetry

Tiny Dreams, Sprouting Tall

Poems about the United States

by Laura Purdie Salas

Capstone press

Mankato, Minnesota

2

Majestic

Eagle

Talons tucked back

Eyes scanning land below

Glossy brown wings riding thermals

Soaring

Happy Birthday to Us!

The Fourth of July's
my favorite day
A big birthday bash
for the U.S. of A.

I stay up real late
'til the sky's full of night
to watch fireworks blooming
and sizzling bright

I'm sad when it's over
and smoke drifts away
The Fourth of July was
my favorite day

4

Lady Liberty

Liberty carries a golden torch

She wears a copper skin

She's broken free of all her chains

and sways upon the wind

Grand Canyon

rock

hard, red

rising, rippling, towering

water flowing, canyon growing

carving, wearing, eroding

sunken, brown

river

Welcome, Rain

Coax the clouds
to gather, darken
Sing the rain
to slant through sky

Turn the earth
to rich black soil
We rejoice when
heavens cry

Louis Armstrong, jazz musician

I Am Jazz

Music

Sweet and soulful

Born in America

Wailing with misery and joy

That's jazz!

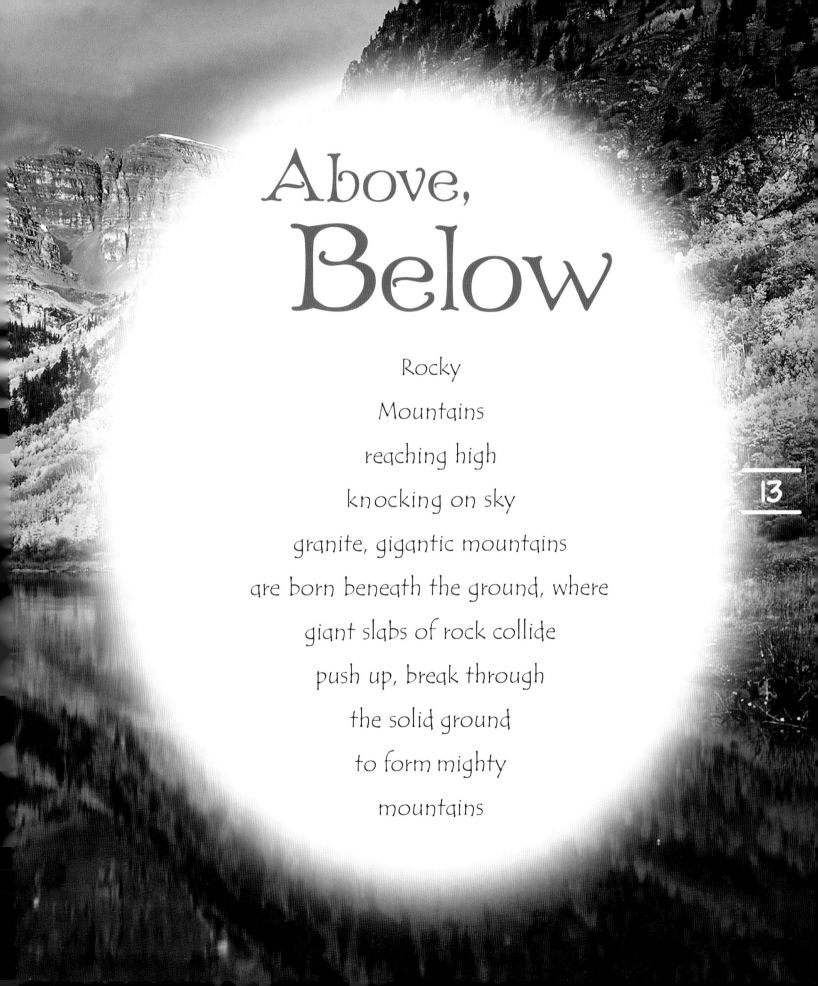

Above,
Below

Rocky

Mountains

reaching high

knocking on sky

granite, gigantic mountains

are born beneath the ground, where

giant slabs of rock collide

push up, break through

the solid ground

to form mighty

mountains

13

Flag Music

Luff-luff-luff
like a clipper's great sail

Rat-a-tat-tat
Like a stormy day's hail

Creak up and down
Like squeaky old brakes

No matter the sound
that our flag outside makes

Still day or windy

Quiet or loud

It makes me feel safer

And stronger and proud

America's Game

We're here for some baseball today!

It's the greatest game that we play!

So hey, batter, swing —

Did you hear the bat sing?

Now that ball's landed six blocks away!

17

Lighthouse on Duty

Guiding

ships that carry

grain, salt, and iron ore

across the Great Lakes, from port to

far shore

Dare

Dare to say

Race does not matter and

Each person can do

Amazing things. This is

My DREAM!

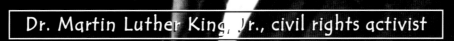

21

Dr. Martin Luther King, Jr., civil rights activist

My Name in Lights

I want to go to Hollywood
I want to meet the stars
Where people live in mansions
And drive the coolest cars

I want to go to Hollywood
And see my name in lights
But then I'd miss my sister
And all our stupid fights

I want to visit Hollywood
I wouldn't need to pack
I'd like to see the sights and
Then I'd like to come right back

Mountain Men

We're the founders

We're the blocks

Our country's leaders

Carved in rocks

Of mountains mighty

Mountains long

Americans:

We're granite-strong

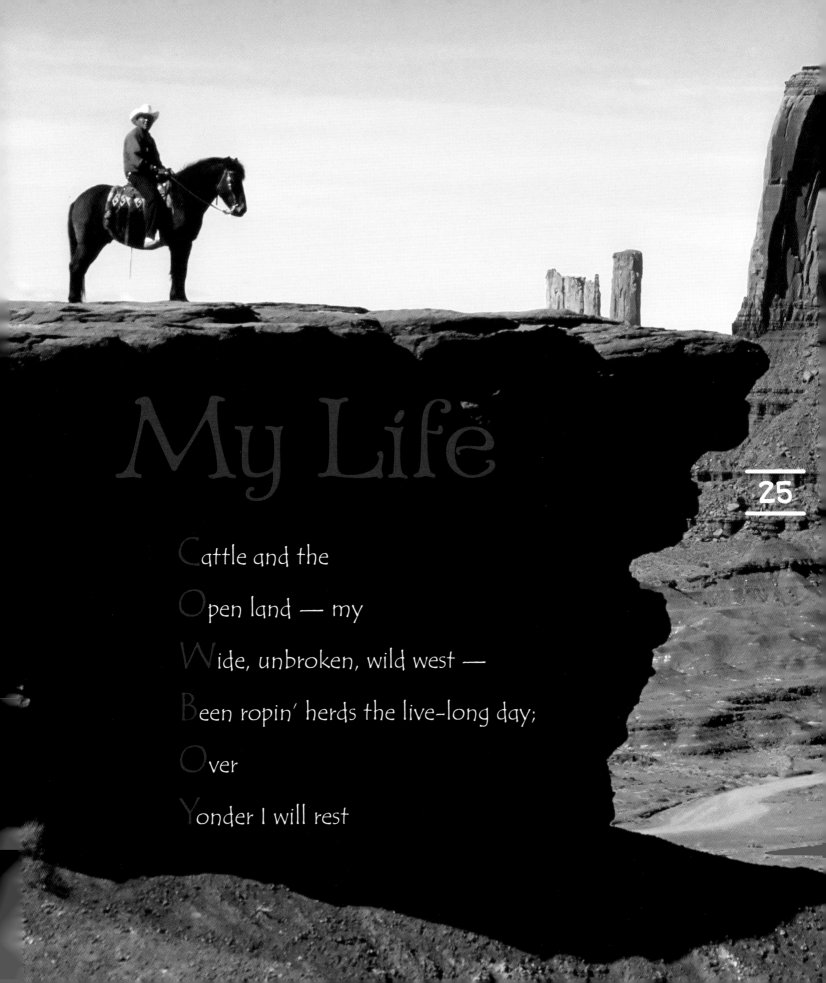

My Life

Cattle and the

Open land — my

Wide, unbroken, wild west —

Been ropin' herds the live-long day;

Over

Yonder I will rest

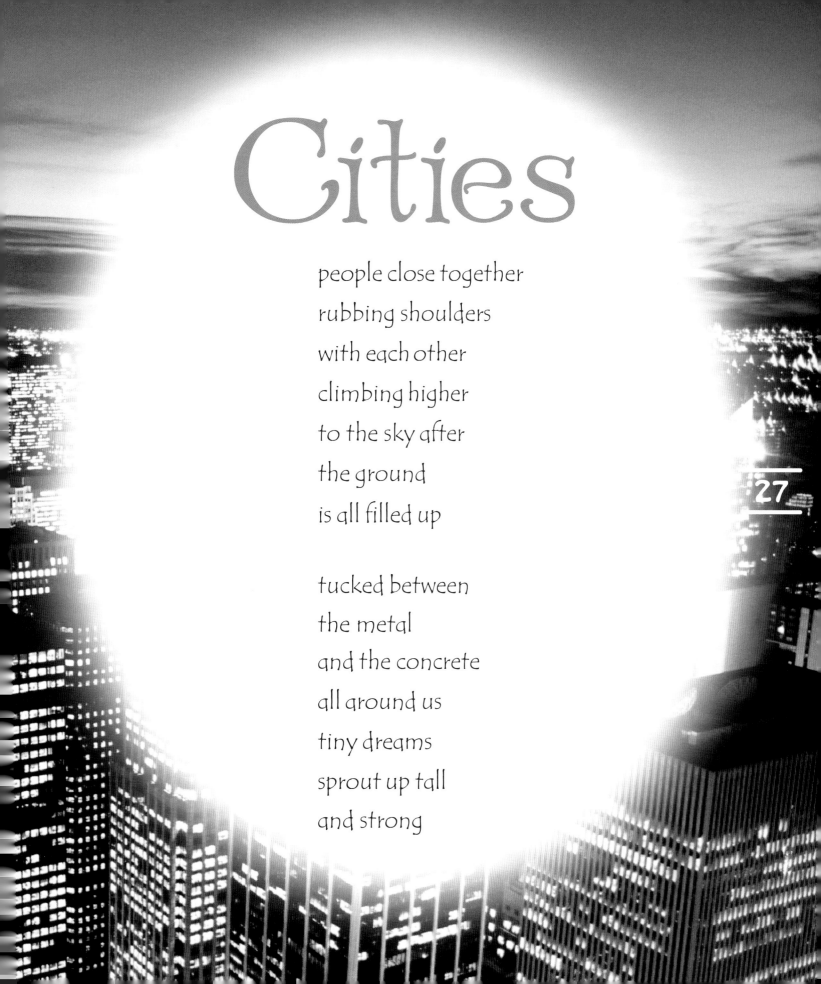

Cities

people close together
rubbing shoulders
with each other
climbing higher
to the sky after
the ground
is all filled up

tucked between
the metal
and the concrete
all around us
tiny dreams
sprout up tall
and strong

The Language of Poetry

28

Alliteration — to have the same beginning sound for several words

Rhyme — to have an end sound that is the same as the end sound of another word

Rhythm — the pattern of beats in a poem

Simile — uses "like" or "as" to say two things are alike

Acrostic

The subject of the poem is written straight down the page. Each line of the poem starts with a letter from the word. "Dare" (page 20) is an acrostic poem.

Cinquain

A poem with five lines. The first line has two syllables. The second line has four, the third has six, the fourth has eight, and the last line has two syllables. "Majestic" (page 3) is an example of a cinquain.

Diamante

A diamond-shaped poem with seven lines. The top half of the poem describes the first word, and the bottom half of the poem describes the last word. "Grand Canyon" (page 7) is a diamante poem.

Free Verse

A poem that does not follow a set pattern or rhythm. It often does not rhyme. "Cities" (page 27) is an example of free verse.

Limerick

A five-line poem that follows a certain rhythm. The first, second, and fifth lines rhyme, and so do the third and fourth lines. "America's Game" (page 16) is a limerick.

Glossary

coax (KOHKS) — to persuade gently and patiently

collide (kuh-LIDE) — to crash together

concrete (KON-kreet) — a hard building material

erode (i-RODE) — to wear away

founder (FOUN-duhr) — someone who sets up or starts something

granite (GRAN-it) — a hard gray rock

Great Lakes (GRAYT LAKES) — a chain of five large lakes in America and Canada

mansion (MAN-shuhn) — a large and grand house

port (PORT) — a place where ships dock or anchor safely

rope (ROHP) — to catch with a lasso or rope

scan (SKAN) — to look at closely and carefully

slab (SLAB) — a broad, flat, thick piece of something

talon (TAL-uhn) — a sharp claw of a bird

thermal (THUR-muhl) — a rising current of warm air

yonder (YON-dur) — over there

Read More

Bates, Katharine. *America, the Beautiful*. New York: G.P. Putnam's Sons, 2003.

Scillian, Devin. *One Nation: America by the Numbers*. Chelsea, Mich.: Sleeping Bear Press, 2002.

Internet Sites

Facthound offers a safe, fun way to find Internet sites related to this book. All of the sites on FactHound have been researched by our staff.

Here's how:

1. Visit *www.facthound.com*

2. Choose your grade level.

3. Type in this book ID **1429612088** for age-appropriate sites. You may also browse subjects by clicking on letters, or by clicking on pictures and words.

4. Click on the **Fetch It** button.

FactHound will fetch the best sites for you!

Index of Poems

Above, Below, 13

America's Game, 16

Cities, 27

Dare, 20

Flag Music, 15

Grand Canyon, 7

Happy Birthday to Us!, 4

I Am Jazz, 11

Lady Liberty, 5

Lighthouse on Duty, 19

Majestic, 3

Mountain Men, 24

My Life, 25

My Name in Lights, 23

Welcome, Rain, 8

32

A+ Books are published by Capstone Press,
151 Good Counsel Drive, P.O. Box 669, Mankato, Minnesota 56002.
www.capstonepress.com

1 2 3 4 5 6 13 12 11 10 09 08

Library of Congress Cataloging-in-Publication Data
Salas, Laura Purdie.
    Tiny dreams, sprouting tall: Poems about the United States/by Laura Purdie Salas.
    p. cm. — (A+ books. Poetry)
    Includes bibliographical references and index.
    Summary: "A collection of original, United States-themed poetry for children accompanied by striking photos. The book demonstrates a variety of common poetic forms and defines poetic devices" — Provided by publisher.
    ISBN-13: 978-1-4296-1208-1 (hardcover)
    ISBN-10: 1-4296-1208-8 (hardcover)
    ISBN-13: 978-1-4296-1748-2 (softcover)
    ISBN-10: 1-4296-1748-9 (softcover)
    1. United States — Juvenile poetry. 2. Children's poetry, American. I. Title. II. Series.
PS3619.A4256T56 2008
811'.6 — dc22   2007034887

Credits
Jenny Marks, editor; Ted Williams, designer; Scott Thoms, photo researcher

Photo Credits
Capstone Press/Karon Dubke, 14
Getty Images Inc./Jerome Pollos, 9; Jim Cummins, 16–17; National Geographic/ Stephen St. John, 25; Photographer's Choice/Marvin E. Newman, 26–27
Shutterstock/Emin Kuliyev, 5; gary718, 6; Jason Duplissea, 22; Jason Watson, 2–3; Jonathan Larsen, 24; Joseph, cover, 1, 28; July Flower, 18–19; Steve Reed, 4
SuperStock, Inc./SuperStock, 10, 21
Visuals Unlimited/Adam Jones, 12–13

Note to Parents, Teachers, and Librarians
Tiny Dreams, Sprouting Tall: Poems about the United States uses colorful photographs and a nonfiction format to introduce children to poetry and celebrate the United States. This book is designed to be read independently by an early reader or to be read aloud to a pre-reader. The images help early readers and listeners understand the poems and concepts discussed. The book encourages further learning by including the following sections: The Language of Poetry, Glossary, Read More, Internet Sites, and Index. Early readers may need assistance using these features.